THE CHRISTIAN EXPERIENCE SERIES is for people who are interested in knowing more about their religion, and also for those who have not as yet seen any reason to be interested.

Each booklet in the series provides material for personal thought about, and group discussion of, a basic question which concerns everyone but is seldom openly discussed. Christians are supposed to have the answers to such questions. But the answers they learned in childhood are perhaps no longer satisfactory to them or meaningful to their non-Christian neighbors.

Progress in the "sacred sciences" and in philosophy and the behavioral sciences all shed light on basic questions such as:

Are suffering and death necessary as part of human life?

What is love, anyway?

Is God vanishing from our secular world?

How do we know when we are doing right?

Is Christian hope a hope for "pie in the sky when you die"?

The purpose of the series is not to offer a complete treatment of each question or any ready answers. It is, rather, to suggest lines of thought and perhaps of action that may help the reader to bring religion and life together.

The books in the Christian Experience Series are designed for use in CCD and other groups. Each book contains eight chapters with discussion questions. Each chapter can serve as material for one meeting or two, so that the entire booklet may be used for an eight-week or a sixteen-week season.

Titles in print:

THROUGH DEATH TO LIFE, by Mary Perkins Ryan

ABOUT LOVING, by Rev. David P. O'Neill

"WHERE IS YOUR GOD?", by Donald P. Gray

HOW DO I KNOW I'M DOING RIGHT? Toward the Formation of a Christian Conscience, by Rev. Gerard Sloyan

ABOUT HOPING, by L. Edward Allemand

WHAT DO WE REALLY BELIEVE? by Richard P. McBrien

General Editor, Mary Perkins Ryan

Consultant, Gerard Pottebaum

Sponsored by the National Center of the Confraternity of Christian Doctrine, 1312 Massachusetts Ave., N.W., Washington, D.C.

what do we really believe?

CHRISTIAN EXPERIENCE SERIES NO. 6

what do we really believe?

Rev. Richard P. McBrien

WITNESS BOOKS

 GEO. A. PFLAUM, PUBLISHER
38 WEST FIFTH STREET • DAYTON, OHIO 45402

ACKNOWLEDGMENT

These chapters are adapted from Rev. Richard P. McBrien's columns in *The Catholic Transcript* (Hartford, Conn.), which are syndicated in several other diocesan papers.

The Scripture quotations used in this publication are from the *Revised Standard Version of the Bible,* Copyright 1946 and 1952 by the Division of Christian Education, National Council of the Churches of Christ in the U.S.A., and used by permission.

PHOTO CREDITS

Cover and text, Paul Tucker.

NIHIL OBSTAT

Rev. John J. Stack
Censor Delegatus

IMPRIMATUR

Most Reverend Henry J. O'Brien, D.D.
Archbishop of Hartford
October 2, 1968

The Nihil Obstat and Imprimatur are official declarations that a book or pamphlet is free of doctrinal or moral error. No implication is contained therein that those who have granted the Nihil Obstat and Imprimatur agree with the contents, opinions or statements expressed.

Library of Congress Catalog Card Number: 69-20295

FOREWORD

To feel threatened in one's faith seems to be a fairly common aspect of Christian experience today, especially perhaps among Catholics. Many are deeply disturbed because what they were taught, both about what to believe and how to practice their faith, seems to be open to question and change. Many others think they are losing their faith because they find that what they were taught as "the Faith" and the way to practice it seems, not merely irrelevant, but even positively opposed to authentic human living.

Both these kinds of Catholics assume that the presentation of the faith in which they were brought up is the only possible one. But, as Fr. McBrien points out in this booklet, *no* presentation of the faith ever has been or ever could be the only final and authentic one. Any such presentation, including the one epitomized in the Baltimore Catechism, is necessarily the product of a particular theological perspective and conditioned by many human factors. It is one way of understanding and expressing the Christian faith, but not that faith itself. The presentation of the faith with which American Catholics have been familiar can, therefore, be changed, and it needs to be changed since its inadequacy to the Church's developing understanding of the faith has become evident.

This booklet clarifies the change in perspective as to how we look at the central affirmations of our faith, inaugurated by Vatican II, and what this change implies in the practical conduct of Catholics' lives. It should therefore help those readers who felt secure with the old perspective to find the new one full of promise, not threat. And it should help readers who are unhappy with the old perspective to realize that, in rejecting it, they need not reject the faith; they can discover it afresh.

Mary Perkins Ryan

CONTENTS

what do we really believe?

Chapter One

CAN "THE FAITH" CHANGE?

For the Spirit searches everything, even the depths of God. For what person knows a man's thoughts except the spirit of the man which is in him? So also no one comprehends the thoughts of God except the Spirit of God. Now we have received not the spirit of the world, but the Spirit which is from God, that we might understand the gifts bestowed on us by God. And we impart this in words not taught by human wisdom but taught by the Spirit, interpreting spiritual truths to those who possess the Spirit. The unspiritual man does not receive the gifts of the Spirit of God, for they are folly to him, and he is not able to understand them because they are spiritually discerned. The spiritual man judges all things, but is himself to be judged by no one. "For who has known the mind of the Lord so as to instruct him?" But we have the mind of Christ.

1 Cor. 2:10-16

During a general audience in April, 1968, and again at the close of the Year of Faith in June, Pope Paul VI issued a fatherly rebuke to those who dare to distort Church dogma. He insisted that the Second Vatican Council provides no basis for "dangerous and at times foolhardy interpretations and distortions of traditional Catholic doctrine."

One cannot easily disagree with the Pope's point of view. It is a matter of self-evident truth that distortions of the Catholic faith are always a bad thing, especially when they are deliberate or foolhardy.

But some Catholics automatically assume that, when the Pope speaks in this fashion, the thrust of his remarks is against the liberal wing of the Church alone. His words, however, apply just as directly to the other side of the ecclesiastical spectrum, to those who openly and actively resist every new interpretation of Catholic doctrine and every new proposal for pastoral reform as if they were the fabrication of Satan. Such people assume, all the while, that *their* understanding of Catholic dogma, *their* particular brand of theology, is the *only* orthodox position. Arrogance is not the private preserve of any single group in the Church.

It must be emphasized again and again that theology is not faith. Theology is a product of human reasoning; faith is a gift of God. Theology attempts a verbal explanation of faith, but it can neither create faith nor destroy it. Theology is, simply put, "faith seeking understanding" (St. Anselm).

It would be idolatrous to exalt theology to the level of faith, to suggest that one particular understanding of the Gospel is the *only* legitimate expression. And it is precisely this assumption that we must continually call into question. It should, in fact, be apparent by now that the so-called "traditional theology" (i.e., the theology which prevailed in Catholic seminaries, colleges, and parochial schools through most of the anti-Modernist era, from the beginning of this century until the post-World War II period) does not do full justice to the Christian faith. Indeed, no theology can do full justice to the Christian faith—not even the theology that permeates this booklet.

The Church has nothing to fear from people who make errors in theology, because theological error cannot destroy the Body of Christ. What hampers her work more than occasional mistakes in research and writing is the attitude of some of her members who insist that there is only one way

to interpret and to explain the Catholic faith—
their own. (And may God have mercy on the
souls of those who dare to disagree with them!)

Undoubtedly there are still some biblical fundamentalists in the Catholic Church today, but no
one—not even the self-professed defenders of
orthodoxy—can find official support for their
position. In fact, the battleground has shifted
from Scripture (remember the vacuous debates
about the star in the East, the Magi, and the
Angel Gabriel?) to dogma. And biblical fundamentalism has given way to doctrinal fundamentalism.

The Council of Trent *said* such-and-such;
therefore, Trent meant such-and-such. No attempt to examine the statement in its proper
context. No attempt to deal with the problem of
language and the influence of contemporary philosophy. No attempt to investigate the theological
point at issue, nor the actual position of those
whom the Church apparently sought to repudiate.
No attempt to determine the amount of teaching
authority which the particular doctrinal statement was intended to have. No attempt to see
how this same doctrinal statement might be re-
thought and recast in terms which we, some four
centuries later, might more appropriately understand.

Yet why should doctrinal statements be any

more "literally" true than scriptural ones? Why
should we be reluctant to apply to dogmatic definitions of past councils the same standards of
interpretation that we have applied to the Word
of God itself?

The simple truth is that we claimed too much
for our theologies in the past. We imposed upon
ourselves and others intellectual demands we had
no right to impose. We proposed something as
"certain" that we should have proposed as "prob-
able" or "likely." The only mature attitude now
is to acknowledge our excesses, accept the con-
sequences, and resolve to learn by our past
mistakes. We must confront the Gospel anew,
with new ways of approaching reality and with
new modes of expression.

The purpose of this booklet, therefore, is two-
fold: (1) to raise some questions about past and
present formulations of faith; and (2) to offer
some suggestions for a genuinely contemporary
understanding of the Gospel. This booklet is
not intended to be a comprehensive presentation
of Catholic teaching, as if in competition with the
Dutch Catechism or any such volume. The reader
will discover that many doctrines are not treated
at all. We are concerned here with central affirmations of the Catholic faith, in an effort to help our
readers begin to articulate an answer to the question: what do we *really* believe?

This question can be taken in one of two ways:
(1) What notions do many Catholics *actually*
have about the Gospel? and (2) What *should*
the Gospel really mean to the Catholic of today?

I shall consider the first meaning of the question at once, by submitting a summary description of the theological mentality of many contemporary Catholics:

"In the beginning, God existed in trinitarian
solitude. Then, for reasons best known to himself, he decided to create something. The summit
of this creation was man, whom he made into his
own image and likeness. He provided the first
man and woman with every kind of gift and
comfort. This was truly man's golden age.

"But God felt that he had to test our first
parents to see if they were really worthy of his
trust and love. As all the world knows, Adam and
Eve failed miserably. They spoiled everything
for us, then and for all time. Having insulted the
majesty of the almighty Lord of the universe,
they could do nothing by themselves to repair the
damage. God, an infinite being, had been injured.
Only an infinite being could make reparation for
the offense. (The terrible deed they committed
we call 'original sin.')

"Mercifully, God gave us a second chance.
He announced that he would eventually send his
only-begotten Son from heaven to earth. The Son

would offer himself as a sacrificial lamb to repair the infinite damage committed against the dignity of God.

"And so Jesus Christ came among us from heaven to make up for that mysterious sin which Adam and Eve committed back there at the dawn of human history. The wrath of God had to be appeased, and his very own Son was chosen for the task. Jesus went to Calvary because his Father in heaven demanded his death in payment for our sins.

"Jesus' work did not end on the cross, however. He rose from the dead to prove that he was truly the Son of God, so that men would always believe in him and follow his commandments. For by believing in him and by following his commandments, each man can save his own immortal soul.

"Jesus did not intend to remain on earth after his resurrection. He returned to his Father in heaven. (We call this 'the Ascension.') But before that, he established a Church which would carry on his work and in which he would still be present (especially in the Blessed Sacrament, distributed as Communion and reserved in the tabernacle).

"The Church continues the work of bringing men into contact with Christ and of saving souls by administering the seven sacraments. These sacraments are valid means of grace because they are performed by people in the Church who have been given the power to celebrate them. We call these men 'priests.'

"The priests, in turn, are valid ministers of the sacraments because they have been ordained by bishops. And bishops, in turn, are valid leaders because they are successors of the Twelve Apostles, which means that they can trace their holy orders all the way back, in an unbroken chain, to the time of the Apostles themselves. It is the Pope who decides which priests will become bishops.

"The Pope, finally, is the 'Vicar of Christ' because he is the successor of Peter and he, too, can trace his papal power back through history. Unlike the rest of the people in the Church, he is infallible. What the Pope says, goes.

"At some point in the future, Christ is going to come back from heaven in order to wind things up. (The world by that time will be in flames.) All those who believed what the Church taught and who obeyed what the Church commanded will be saved; the rest (at least those who openly resisted the Church) will be consigned to hell for all eternity. And this is only just."

I submit that this is no frivolous caricature. It represents the "faith" of many sincere people.

The task of disengaging the Gospel from these assorted ideas is an urgent one for all of us.

DISCUSSION QUESTIONS

What is the difference between faith, theology, and doctrine? Can you think of anything that was once proposed to you as a matter of faith that is now accepted as a matter of theology alone?

How widespread is the notion of Catholic "faith" which is summarized in the second half of this chapter? Before reading the rest of this booklet, determine what is objectionable and what is acceptable in the summary of beliefs.

Which of the "objectionable" beliefs do you think is the most serious and has the widest currency among your own family, friends, and acquaintances? In what way does this belief affect the overall religious mentality of these people?

Do you think that booklets of this kind and the discussion in which you are now engaged really do any good? Or is it simply one of the many harmless games that Catholics like to play? How can the theological reorientation stimulated by this booklet and these discussions contribute to the renewal and reform of the Church, and particularly your own local parish community?

But, as it is written, "What no eye has seen, nor ear heard, nor the heart of man conceived, what God has prepared for those who love him," God has revealed to us through the Spirit. For the Spirit searches everything, even the depths of God. For what person knows a man's thoughts except the spirit of the man which is in him? So also no one comprehends the thoughts of God except the Spirit of God.

1 Cor. 2:9-11

Chapter Two

WHAT KIND OF A GOD?

For it is always in thy power to show great strength, and who can withstand the might of thy arm? Because the whole world before thee is like a speck that tips the scales, and like a drop of morning dew that falls upon the ground. But thou art merciful to all, for thou canst do all things, and thou dost overlook men's sins, that they may repent. For thou lovest all things that exist, and hast loathing for none of the things which thou hast made, for thou wouldst not have made anything if thou hadst hated it. How would anything have endured if thou hadst not willed it? Or how would anything not called forth by thee have been preserved. Thou sparest all things, for they are thine, O Lord who lovest the living.

Wis. 11:21-26

When a Christian theologian (be he Catholic or Protestant) suggests a rethinking of our faith, he is sometimes accused of diluting or accommodating the truth in order to make it acceptable to the nonbeliever. Today's theologian could hardly improve upon the response given by the late Anglican Archbishop of York, William Temple: "I am not asking, What will Jones swallow? I am Jones, asking what there is to eat."

The abiding concern of the contemporary Christian theologian is not so to water down the traditional doctrines that nearly everybody can swallow them. The theologian is trying to be honest to himself, and honest to the Church. His immediate responsibility is to the Christian community, within which and for which he does his theology, and to himself as an integral part of that community.

Through its theological reflections, the Church of every age must put to itself the perennial questions of Christian faith: Who is God? What is sin? Who is Christ? What is redemption and salvation? Why the Church? In brief, what do we *really* believe?

A faith that cannot tolerate constant criticism

is no longer the "good news of salvation." It has
become an ossified relic of some past and alien
culture. On the contrary, the Christian faith
must always be the new wine. But new wine cannot be "put into old wineskins; if it is, the skins
burst, and the wine is spilled, and the skins are
destroyed; but new wine is put into fresh wineskins, and so both are preserved" (Mt. 9:17).

We do not have to endorse the radical conclusions of the "death-of-God" theologians in
order to give them proper credit for recognizing
and dramatizing some real weaknesses in our
"common-sense" concepts about God. (And so
often those who are most vociferous in defense
of the element of "mystery" seem to be committed
with equal passion to a kind of "common-sense"
theology.)

When all is said and done, what do we really
believe about God? Do we believe that life is a
kind of game that God is playing? That the earth
and all of human history is but a sporting arena
where God tests us, one by one? Do we really
believe that God put the first two human beings
to some kind of examination, and that because
they failed it, he decided to punish them—and
not only them, but every man, in every age, in
every human situation?

Do we really believe that his sense of justice
functions with metaphysical inevitability and pre-

cision? That he can never be crossed? That he never forgets an "insult"? Do we really believe that God needs and demands our worship? That like some kind of Oriental potentate, he craves for human affection and homage?

Do we really believe that God stands idly by when men suffer and die? Do we believe that he deliberately sends cancer to little children or removes a mother from a young family so as to give us all a more intimate share in the cross? Do we really believe this? Is this the God of our faith?

Do we really believe that God makes the sun shine, or the rain to fall? That prayers before the big game or the family picnic will dictate the kind of weather (or the kind of result) he will produce?

Do we really believe that God sent his only Son from heaven to earth in order to die? Do we really believe that God wants anyone to die?

Do we really believe that God chooses to speak to mankind only through one organization (the Church) or through one human being (the Pope)? Do we really believe that God speaks only to Christians (or to Catholics) and to no one else? That what the others get, they get from us?

Do we really believe that God is always on our side, that he, too, despises all Communists and all who seem to war against the Church? That

he, too, is only on the side of "law and order?"

What do we *really* believe about God? If we believe any of *these* things, and if they are distortions of Christian belief, then where do we go, how do we find out about the real God, "The God and Father of our Lord Jesus Christ"?

We need above all to reflect on the portrait of God which emerges from reflection on the testimony of Sacred Scripture. The pages of the Bible cannot finally resolve metaphysical questions about God (whether he is Pure Act, Primordial Being, the Ground of Being, Processive Being, etc.), but they do set limits and establish norms for any such philosophical speculation.

The late French novelist Albert Camus described God as the eternal bystander whose back is turned to the woe of this world. We Christians may recoil from his description, insisting that it is a mere caricature of our faith. And yet we must confess that it is not always easy, even for us, to disengage the God of the Gospel from the God of "common-sense" Christian belief.

Whatever we may believe about God, it cannot contradict the clear and essential teaching of the New Testament (and particularly the first epistle of St. John) that God is love. The superstitious and the vindictive are never comfortable with this description, but one simply cannot improve upon it.

God loves us as a Father, for "In him we live and move and have our being" (Acts 17:28). His most distinctive characteristic is his faithfulness to what he has promised. He is, so to speak, a man of his word, and the word that he has uttered has been consistently a word of love and friendship. "I, the Lord your God, hold your right hand; it is I who say to you, 'Fear not, I will help you'" (Is. 41:13).

The God of our faith is the God of Jesus of Nazareth. "He who has seen (him) has seen the Father" (Jn. 14:9). As St. Paul insists again and again, "God was in Christ, reconciling the world to himself" (2 Cor. 5:19). For God "has loathing for none of the things which thou has made" (Wis. 11:24).

Because God is like this, he, too, struggles against pain and suffering and death. He can be pleased by nothing that strikes against the spirit and dignity of man. For God is still in Christ, reconciling the world to himself: giving sight to the blind, hearing to the deaf, health to the lame, hope to the poor, life to the dead (Lk. 4:18-19).

But by human standards his strategy is too kind. He has chosen to encounter us and to collaborate with us in that unique symbol of love of others, Jesus of Nazareth. Through his anointed one, God reveals his love in humble service.

For the Lord came not to be served, but to serve (Mk. 10:45), and he emptied himself for us unto death (Phil. 2:5-11). God thereby confounds the mighty and the proud.

This is the God of our faith; this is the only God in whom we can believe and whom we can serve with gladness and gratitude. It is he who gives meaning, direction and purpose to our lives and to our history. It is he who invites us to collaborate with him, in freedom, to build the Kingdom of God: a Kingdom of truth and justice, of charity and peace.

The God of the Gospel is essentially "for us," in the sense of willing the fullness of well-being for all men. He reveals this in his Son who is the "Christ for us." To live for God means to live for others. "If any one has the world's goods and sees his brother in need, yet closes his heart against him, how does God's love abide in him?" (1 Jn. 3:17).

And to live for others is to live "in Christ." This is the whole point of Christian existence. Either we believe this, or Christian existence is a sham. To recall Camus' imagery, we Christians would become eternal bystanders with backs turned to the woe of this world.

Membership in the Church makes sense only in terms of our relationship to *this* God: the God

of the Gospel and the God of Jesus Christ. It is
to the extension of *his* Kingdom that we have
committed ourselves in Baptism.

DISCUSSION QUESTIONS

Do you think that most Catholics honestly
confront the problem of belief? To use Archbishop Temple's remark, do you think they put
themselves in the place of "Jones" or do you
think many Catholics simply wonder why so many
other people do not accept Catholicism?

Is there really a need to rethink the Gospel in
every new period of the Church's history? Can
you give any examples of how changes in the intellectual or cultural climate have brought about
changes in the understanding of the Christian
faith? Is it possible that Christians could actually
compromise or distort the faith while trying to
accomodate it to new situations? Do you think
this is a danger today?

If we accepted the ideas about God mentioned
in the first half of this chapter, how would our
ideas about the redemption, the Church, and the
sacraments be affected?

Do you think that Camus' criticism of the
Christian belief about God is a fair one? Do you
think many people really think this way? In what
way would this concept of God be harmful?

Why do so many religious people believe that God causes evil, "sends suffering," etc.? Do you think that we should re-examine our ideas about some of God's attributes: e.g., his omnipotence?

Beloved, if God so loved us, we also ought to love one another. No man has ever seen God; if we love one another, God abides in us and his love is perfected in us. By this we know that we abide in him and he in us, because he has given us of his own Spirit. And we have seen and testify that the Father has sent his Son as the Savior of the world. Whoever confesses that Jesus is the Son of God, God abides in him, and he in God. So we know and believe the love God has for us. God is love, and he who abides in love abides in God, and God abides in him. In this is love perfected with us, that we may have confidence for the day of judgment, because as he is so are we in this world. There is no fear in love, but perfect love casts out fear. For fear has to do with punishment, and he who fears is not perfected in love. We love, because he first loved us. If any one says, "I love God," and hates his brother, he is a liar; for he who does not love his brother whom he has seen, cannot love God whom he has not seen. And this commandment we have from him, that he who loves God should also love his brother.

1 John 4:11-21

Chapter Three

ATONEMENT VS. AT-ONE-MENT

His divine power has granted to us all things that pertain to life and godliness, through the knowledge of him who called us to his own glory and excellence, by which he has granted to us his precious and very great promises, that through these you may escape from the corruption that is in the world because of passion, and become partakers of the divine nature. For this very reason make every effort to supplement your faith with virtue, and virtue with knowledge, and knowledge with self-control and self-control with steadfastness, and steadfastness with godliness, and godliness with brotherly affection, and brotherly affection with love. For if these things are yours and abound, they keep you from being ineffective or unfruitful in the knowledge of our Lord Jesus Christ. For whoever lacks these things is blind and shortsighted and has forgotten that he was cleansed from his old sins. Therefore, brethren, be the more zealous to confirm your call and election, for if you do this you will never fall; so there will be richly provided for you an entrance into the eternal kingdom of our Lord and Savior Jesus Christ. Therefore I intend always to remind you of these things, though you know them and are established in the truth that you have.

2 Peter 1:3-12

If the God of Scripture, "the God and Father of our Lord Jesus Christ" (2 Cor. 1:3), is the God we are called to believe in, what happens to the ideas of sin and redemption with which we are familiar—ideas which imply quite a different kind of God? Must we continue to believe that God once existed by himself and then decided to create something? Then he tested his creatures to see if they were truly worthy of his trust and love (as if he wouldn't have known this from the start)?

Must we believe that life was perfect at the beginning: no work, no worries, no problems, no responsibilities; perfection of knowledge, perfection of physical resources, perfection of human relationships, perfection of human achievements? That Adam and Eve spoiled it all when they failed the test (not many think there had to be an apple, but a "test?"—yes!)?

Human history, in this view, becomes an arena where each individual man, woman, and child tries to work out his or her own salvation. And because of the sin of our first parents, each one of us has one arm strapped behind his back, so to speak. It is more difficult now to get on with

the business of life because of what *they* did in
the Garden of Eden. Moreover, we cannot achieve
the real purpose of our existence at all unless we
regain the sanctifying grace or "divine life" that
Adam and Eve lost for us and Christ regained for
mankind. This grace given at Baptism—lost by
mortal sin—may be regained by Penance. The
important thing is to *die* in the state of grace and
so be finally saved from eternal damnation.

The Church, therefore, is the place where the
struggle for personal salvation is a good deal
easier to wage. While the rest of men are wander-
ing up this road and down that one, the Church
alone has full possession of the map of life and
"means of grace." Each man remains responsible
for his own individual conduct along the highway,
but if he stays with the Church, at least he will
know that he is heading in the right direction.

But this idea of the Church rests upon certain
presuppositions about creation and original sin
which really cannot easily be sustained.

Creation does not necessarily mean that God
produced everything that now exists, all at once.
The creation-story and the description of the Fall
in Genesis are not intended as scientific or photo-
graphic accounts of the origins of the universe or
of the introduction of evil in the world.

What happens, then, if we suggest that sin is
not something that occurs simply because Adam

and Eve committed a blunder many centuries ago? It seems better to propose that sin is an aspect of the human condition, and that individual sin makes sense only in terms of a man's solidarity with the rest of mankind. For sin entails not only alienation from God, but a disruption in our relationships with one another, and even with the rest of creation. Indeed, we produce alienation from God precisely through this disruption of human relationships. Sin is not so much a question of disobedience to divine commands as it is an attitude or behavior which strikes against the human spirit.*

Of course, sin must have had a beginning, but we do not really know *when* and *how*. We do know, however, that sin is impossible apart from human freedom. As freedom grew in man, so did the possibility of sin.

What we can be sure of is the fact that sin now exists in the world. Our real problem is not so much a question of how and when man first sinned, but the fact that man continues to sin even today.

The Second Vatican Council considerably expanded the limits of the discussion about original sin and redemption when it acknowledged, with apparent approval, that "the human race has

---

*The reader may wish to pursue this at greater length. See Karl Rahner, "The Unity of Love of God and Love of Neighbor," in *Theology Digest* (Summer, 1967), pp. 87-93.

passed from a rather static concept of reality to a more dynamic, evolutionary one" (*Pastoral Constitution on the Church in the Modern World,* art. 5, para. 4). This means that man is still growing, and that history is growing with him. Life is not a matter of trying to recover our lost innocence or of keeping on God's good side, but of moving ahead with sober confidence that, in collaboration with him, we can truly recreate the face of this earth.

That is why the Christian must be as acutely concerned about the war in Vietnam, hunger in India, or poverty in our own cities, as he is with worshipping God at Mass or "keeping the commandments of the Church."

The Church is itself a part of a world in evolution. It cannot be committed to the past alone, but to the present and more especially to the future. Its mood must be one of hope rather than nostalgia. Its prayer remains: "Thy Kingdom come!"

It would be difficult to exaggerate the importance of this change of perspective. Being a Christian does not mean having all the answers to life's problems, but having a special responsibility to solve them. Salvation comes to those who struggle for God's Kingdom; it is not simply the reward for "keeping out of trouble" until your "time is up." Salvation and the Kingdom of God are two sides of the same coin. One is saved through his connection with the full human community. Without community, man is dead. That is why Hell is really the extinction of life. It is for those who choose to reject the human community, who wish to "go it alone."

The Kingdom of God is similarly described. It comes into being wherever men and women live according to his will and, therefore, under his reign. And the will of God has been embodied for all time in the preaching and ministry, the death and resurrection, of Jesus of Nazareth: that we should have love one for another. Where there is love, there is community. Where there is community, there is the Kingdom of God in process. And where there is the Kingdom, there is salvation.

But where did we derive our more limited, non-human idea of sin and redemption that has become a part of the conventional "faith" of so many Catholics? The fact is that for almost a thousand years Catholics and Protestants alike have accepted, without question, a theological opinion of St. Anselm, regarding the Incarnation and the Redemption. Anselm argued that God had to become man because man had committed an infinite offense against him, and only an infinite being could repair such damage. Jesus Christ, who is both God and man, died on the cross to pay off mankind's "debt" to the Father.

We did not often stop to ask: What kind of God is it that would demand anyone's death in payment for an offense committed against him? What kind of God would send his only Son to die in "reparation"? Calling it all a "mystery" is simply avoiding the issue.

Significantly, Anselm's *theory*—and that is all it is—does not enjoy the same wide acceptance today as it once did in the past. Some contemporary Christian theologians, however, have gone to the opposite extreme and have reduced the Redemption to a matter of "good example." Jesus came to show us how to live as authentic human beings. If we *imitate* him (and that is the key word), we can be "saved," i.e., we, too, can attain to full manhood.

But in this existential understanding of the Redemption, nothing objective takes place outside of us. What Christ did on the cross (and through his resurrection) does not really mean anything in itself. It only counts if some human being is sufficiently motivated thereby to follow the "example" of Christ.

If we are to maintain some balance in our faith, we cannot responsibly endorse either extreme. An orthodox understanding of the Redemption demands both elements: the objective and the existential.

We must recognize that through the life, death, and glorification of Jesus, God has definitely broken into our history, that he is in Christ reconciling the world to himself by not reckoning against men their sins (2 Cor. 5:19). Fundamentally, the Redemption is something that *God* has done, and is doing, on our behalf.

But the Redemption similarly demands and includes our personal response. (Anselm's theory makes it purely objective.) Through the ministry of Jesus, God is showing us that we need not be enslaved by the principalities and the powers of this world: money, power, superstition, fear, anxiety, etc. Man is liberated in Christ to ascend to the fullness of humanity. Christ has disclosed and released for us the limitless possibilities of the human spirit. To know what this freedom means and then to exercise it is to have been redeemed.

It should be obvious, of course, that the possibilities for such freedom are not restricted to Christians nor are they realized in a single instance, once and for all (e.g., at Baptism). If salvation is a matter of realizing to the fullest one's human potential (but always *in response to* the call of God), its universality becomes self-evident. Every man and woman, by virtue of his or her membership in the human community itself, is confronted with this *responsibility* of hu-

man fulfillment and, therefore, with this opportunity for salvation. Baptism signifies (among other things) the beginning, not the end, of this process. It reminds us that what God is doing in and for his Church, he is doing in and for the whole of mankind.

Given St. Anselm's theory about the Redemption, it is understandable that the Church was seen primarily as an agent of salvation, a means of grace. The Church's job is to keep God happy, so to speak, by offering him sacrifices and prayers, and by seeing to it that his creatures "stay in line."

But in the fuller, more balanced theology of the Redemption, the Church becomes the place where God continues to make himself known in our history. The Church is, first of all, a mystery —the sacrament of God in the world. And the Church is also the community which gives hope to the rest of mankind, reminding all men that the principalities and the powers have been overthrown. Its mission is threefold: to proudly and confidently announce our liberation in Christ (*kerygma:* proclamation); to employ all its resources—moral, cultural, financial, and political —to extend God's Kingdom (*diakonia:* service); to offer itself as an example of what God can accomplish in the world when men are open to his grace (*koinonia:* community).

What, then, do we really believe about Christ and the Redemption? One thing is certain: however firmly it was imbedded in our minds during our years of catechetical formation, we need *not* hold fast to the theory of St. Anselm. To understand this is to have achieved much already.

In this light, we can see how unnecessary are the worries of those who fear that the "sacrificial" aspect of the Mass is being de-emphasized today in favor of its meal aspect, or that the place of "sacrifice" in the Christian life is rapidly passing out of sight and mind.

It is certainly the teaching of the Church, enunciated by the Council of Trent, that "in the divine sacrifice that is offered in the Mass, the same Christ who offered himself once in a bloody manner on the altar of the cross is present and is offered in an unbloody manner."

The key word is "sacrifice." What does it mean? What does the average Catholic understand by it? Does he assume that sacrifice means doing something difficult and distasteful, such as walking rather than riding to church, or giving up desserts, or spending extra time on one's knees, or making a larger contribution to the Sunday collection?

And in what sense is the crucifixion of Jesus a "sacrifice"? I have already suggested that a "traditional" explanation of the Redemption (St.

Anselm's) is just that—an explanation, or a theory. We need not believe that Jesus died on the cross to "pay off a debt" to the Father.

Our understanding of the sacrifice of the cross can therefore be altered, and with it our understanding of the Mass as a sacrifice.

In Sacred Scripture, and particularly in the Old Testament, we can find two fundamentally different ideas of sacrifice: cultic and prophetic. The first was prevalent in the Pentateuch and more specifically in Exodus. In this view, sacrifice is a matter of "burnt offerings." A victim is handed over and destroyed as an act of homage to God. I suspect that many Catholics have this cultic idea in mind when they hear or use the word "sacrifice."

But the cultic concept was superseded by the prophetic idea of sacrifice as martyrdom, or as witnessing. When Jesus characterized himself as the Suffering Servant of God, it was the prophetic (e.g., deutero-Isaian), not the cultic idea of service that he was embracing.

And this was, in fact, the way in which he understood his ministry: "Sacrifices and offerings thou hast not desired, but a body hast thou prepared for me . . . 'Lo, I have come to do thy will, O God' " (Heb. 10:5 ff.). The author of the epistle concludes: "He abolishes the first (i.e., cultic sacrifice) in order to establish the second (i.e., sacrifice of the heart, of a life lived in cooperation with the will of God)."

Thus, Christ's death on the cross exemplifies and fulfills the true meaning and aim of the cultic sacrifices of the Old Law: to establish harmony between God and man. And that harmony exists wherever the will of God and the moral life of man are one. This is what the Redemption accomplishes: an at-one-ment, the initial realization of the Kingdom of God.

Jesus went to the cross because his teachings, his activities, and his very personality put him at odds with the religious establishment of his day. He was a threat to its very existence. He announced the coming of the Kingdom—a kingdom of love, joy, peace, justice, and freedom—while it continued to peddle a program of fear, of legal prescriptions, of slavish fidelity to ritual and custom. The clash was inevitable and Jesus paid the price of his convictions.

His death on the cross was an act of supreme obedience, of subordination of all things (even his very life) to the Kingdom of God. He did not embrace the cross for its own sake, nor because his Father was pushing him relentlessly along the way to Calvary. Rather, he saw this as the inevitable consequence of his life and work. He could not avoid it without compromising his integrity and without retreating from his solemn mission.

Sought after or not the cross became the great sign, the great act of witness to the ultimate meaning and purpose of all human life and of history itself. Only the genuinely free man can save himself, for "he who loses his life shall find it."

Jesus showed us the true relationship between cultic and prophetic sacrifice. The cultic is but the external sign of the underlying reality: a life of dedicated, uncompromising service of others. We have no business laying gifts on the altar as long as our brother has a claim upon us (Mt. 5:23-24). Sacrifice is not for the sake of placating an angry God but of giving him praise and thanks for his goodness, and of reaffirming the mission we all received in Baptism: the reconciliation of all mankind with one another and hence with God.

The Eucharist is this kind of sacrifice. It is the central moment in the life of the Church when the Christian community gathers together and dramatizes its full involvement in the mission of Christ to be the sign and instrument of God's Kingdom. In celebrating the Eucharist, the Church, in effect, puts the world on notice that it has accepted a solemn responsibility—a responsibility accepted by each member in Baptism—

and that it intends to do the best it can to fulfill it. Sacrifice, therefore, makes no sense apart from the mission of the Church to establish and to extend the Kingdom of God. The sensitive Christian will have no trouble finding opportunities to practice it.

The late Dr. Martin Luther King, Jr., provided us with a concrete model of how this theology can look when put into action. As he said so often, "We must meet the forces of hate with the power of love; we must meet physical force with soul force. Our aim must never be to defeat or humiliate the white man, but to win his friendship and understanding."

This is what the redemption is all about: human at-one-ment, not atonement. And that is precisely God's abiding attitude toward us all: not to defeat or humiliate us but to win our friendship and understanding. The resurrection of Jesus remains his promise to us that his love shall prevail.

DISCUSSION QUESTIONS

How does our understanding of original sin influence our ideas about the meaning and direction of human history? What concept of original sin do you think most Catholics have today?

People used to argue a lot about evolution. Do

you think this is still an important question?
Why do you think Teilhard de Chardin has had
such an influence on modern religious thought,
even among non-Christians?

What is sin? Are you satisfied with the "traditional" definitions? Why not?

Has the "Kingdom of God" been a part of your
own catechetical formation? What was your original understanding of this reality? Does it surprise
you to learn that the Kingdom of God was at the
heart and center of the preaching of the Lord?

Do you think that most Catholics still accept
St. Anselm's idea about the Redemption? How
has this theory affected our ideas about God,
Christ, the Church, the sacraments, and especially
the Eucharist?

*Have this mind among yourselves, which
was in Christ Jesus, who, though he was in
the form of God, did not count equality with
God a thing to be grasped, but emptied himself, taking the form of a servant, being born
in the likeness of men. And being found in
human form he humbled himself and became
obedient unto death, even death on a cross.
Therefore God has highly exalted him and
bestowed on him the name which is above
every name, that at the name of Jesus every
knee should bow, in heaven and on earth and*

under the earth, and every tongue confess that Jesus Christ is Lord, to the glory of God the Father.

Phil. 2:5-11

Chapter Four

JESUS IS LORD!—THE CENTRAL AFFIRMATION OF OUR FAITH

He is the image of the invisible God, the firstborn of all creation; for in him all things were created, in heaven and on earth, visible and invisible, whether thrones or dominions or principalities or authorities—all things were created through him and for him. He is before all things, and in him all things hold together. He is the head of the body, the church, he is the beginning, the firstborn from the dead, that in everything he might be pre-eminent. For in him all the fulness of God was pleased to dwell, and through him to reconcile to himself all things, whether on earth or in heaven, making peace by the blood of his cross.

Col. 1:15-20

I should expect very few Catholics, priests or laymen, to be able to point to any extensive treatment of the resurrection in the theology they learned some years ago. Indeed, whenever the resurrection was a topic for study, it was usually in an apologetical framework: Jesus is the Son of God, and he proved this by his miracles and especially his resurrection from the dead. The resurrection of Jesus was not regarded as an essential part of the Redemption. The full saving act took place on the cross (St. Anselm again!); the resurrection was a kind of epilogue.*

Now that we have rejected the idea of the crucifixion as cultic sacrifice and of the Redemption as the payment of a debt owed to God, we are free to view the resurrection of Jesus at the very heart of our Christian faith ("Jesus is Lord!").

The Redemption is the work of the Father, and it is the Father who raised Jesus from the dead for our salvation (Rom. 4:24; 8:11; 10:9; 1 Cor. 6:14; 13:4; Gal. 1:1; Eph. 1:20; Phil. 2:9; 1 Thes. 1:10; 1:21). This is the consistent tradition of Pauline theology, although it has not always

---

*For a fuller consideration, see Avery Dulles, S.J., *Apologetics and the Biblical Christ*, (Newman, Glen Rock, N.J.), Chapter IV.

been part of our catechetical formation. (Some evidence of this lack emerged in the emotional distress manifested by some Catholics when they learned that the newer translations of the Gospels spoke of Jesus being "raised" from the dead rather than "rising" from the dead.)

We are, in fact, saved by the resurrection of Jesus. It is through his resurrection that he communicates the new life of the Spirit to us (Rom. 4:24-25). We are reborn in the Spirit because Jesus has been raised and glorified (Jn. 7:39; 16:7; 20:22; 1 Pet. 1:3-4). Death no longer has a final hold over any one of us. The hope of our own resurrection is founded on our faith in Christ's (1 Cor. 15).*

When the resurrection is torn from the mystery of our Redemption and regarded solely as a proof for the divinity of Jesus, then it can have no real meaning for the life and mission of the Church. But the fact is that its faith is an Easter faith, its mission an Easter mission. We Christians believe that human life and history can and will succeed because Jesus of Nazareth is the risen Lord. The resurrection is the ultimate promise of God that his Kingdom will be brought to perfection for us.

Jesus has left the tomb and gone into the city. He can and must be found there. It is the

---

*For an up-to-date discussion of this new life in the Spirit, see Thomas Sartory, "Changes in Christian Spirituality," in *Life in the Spirit* (H. Kung, ed.), N.Y.: Sheed & Ward, 1968, pp. 57-105.

Church's responsibility to locate him again and again, and release the Spirit which he possesses. The Church is his resurrection community and, as such, a symbol of hope to the world. This is the essence of the Easter message and the task of the Easter faith.

If the resurrection is thus central in the Christian faith and human history, it must obviously have been a real event. But we need to avoid the extremes both of fundamentalism and demythologizing in our understanding of this real event.

Do we really have to believe that the resurrection of Jesus is an historical event in the sense that his goings-about on Easter Sunday could have been recorded on camera if one were available? Some Catholic theologians have come to the conclusion that the answer is very probably "No." The clearest expression of this view has been produced recently by G. G. O'Collins, S. J., of Cambridge University.*

Father O'Collins notes the renewal of interest in the resurrection on the part of Protestant theologians. (Those of my readers who follow the progress of theological discussion through the pages of *The New York Times* and the news magazines will know by now that the new "theology of hope," proposed by Jurgen Moltmann

---

* "Is the Resurrection an 'Historical' Event?" in *Heythrop Journal* (October, 1967; pp. 381-7).

and others, accords a central place to the resurrection of Jesus.) But Father O'Collins finds that
some of the newer Protestant thinking, far from
being "liberal," insists too strongly on the *historical* character of the resurrection. It is such an
event, they suggest, that an historian could verify
it by his own scientific methods.

However, an event cannot be called "historical"
unless it meets certain conditions: (1) its causality must be open to scientific examination; (2)
the event must have been witnessed by impartial
observers; and (3) the event should bear some
relationship to the kind of happenings we com-
monly experience. The resurrection fails to pass
this test: (1) we cannot investigate its causality,
because the Scriptures themselves do not attempt
to give an account, let alone a precise and de-
tailed account, of how it occurred; (2) only be-
lievers testified to the appearances of the Lord;
(3) the resurrection bears no analogy to our
common experience.

In brief, an "historical" event is one that happens in the realm of *space* and *time*. On that
basis, Father O'Collins concludes that the resurrection is not an "historical" event. By his resurrection Christ entered the *new mode* of existence
of the glorified body, a Spirit-filled existence in
which he is the source of life for mankind (2
Cor. 3:17; 1 Cor. 15:43 ff.). For the most part,

his glorified existence is only to be described in negatives: immortal, impassible, etc. "If in fact Christ on the far side of the resurrection continued to exist under the bodily conditions which we experience and within which the historian operates, he would not be the risen Christ."*

Thus the *real event* of the resurrection is central to our redemption in Christ and yet we need not regard it as an *"historical"* event in the strict sense of the word. We can easily see that the resurrection of Jesus differs from the other raisings from the dead mentioned in the Gospels: e.g., the young man from Naim (Lk. 7:11-17), Jairus' daughter (Mk. 5:35-43), and Lazarus (Jn. 11). First, these events are described in some detail, whereas the resurrection of Jesus took place "in the silence of God" (St. Ignatius of Antioch). Secondly, there was never a problem of identification regarding the risen Lazarus or the risen daughter of Jairus, for example; whereas we have several instances in the Gospels where even his disciples failed to recognize the risen Lord.

But the major contrast lies in the fact that the daughter of Jairus and the others resumed their lives under normal bodily conditions and would eventually die again. They had not yet entered into the final state of their existence. Jesus, on the other hand, does not return to our

*Ibid. p. 385.

space-time condition. With his death and burial
his historical existence was completed. He has
moved into his final state of existence where he is
now Spirit (2 Cor. 3:17; see also 1 Cor. 15:
43 ff.). Wherever people catch something of the
contagious quality of his freedom, i.e., wherever
people become friends, there is Jesus. The resurrection happened once-and-for-all for Jesus, but
it happens again and again for other men and
women. It happens whenever the Gospel takes
hold of the hearts of men and shapes their asso-
ciations into a genuine human community.

But this does not in the least mean that the resurrection was not "for real," that our faith is
founded on an illusion. Something objective did
happen on Easter Sunday and its effects have
manifested themselves ever since. The apostles
themselves proclaimed the resurrection of Jesus
as a real event, because they experienced and
understood it as such. St. Paul would even argue
that without the resurrection our faith is in vain
and we are still in our sins (1 Cor. 15:17).

The apostles were convinced that Jesus had
appeared to them at definite times and in specific
places and to a particular number of persons.
These events were not regarded simply as mys-
tical experiences and certainly not as hallucina-
tions. On the contrary, "these appearances are
historical from the side of those who encountered

the risen Lord, but not from the side of Christ himself."*

The resurrection and subsequent appearances are not subject to verification by the objective historian, and yet they are real events. This means that we must believe not only in the redemptive value of the resurrection, but also in the event itself. This is not true, however, in the case of the crucifixion. While faith is required to see the cross as the tree of life, faith is *not* required to accept it as an historical fact. Jesus of Nazareth was crucified, and an historian can verify this. But this is not so with regard to the resurrection. And yet the resurrection is just as *real* as the crucifixion. "Reality" comprises more than what is narrowly regarded as "historical." In other words, one can accept the resurrection as a real, bodily event, without necessarily calling it "historical." I say "necessarily" because there are theologians today (and they are not all fundamentalists) who continue to insist on the strict historicity of the resurrection.

Thus, while there may be room for discussion on the precise meaning of "historical," it must be clear that no Christian can responsibly deny the *reality* of the resurrection. It is something that really happened to Jesus of Nazareth and not merely to his disciples and apostles (as Bultmann

Ibid. p. 386.

has suggested). Indeed, the reality of the resurrection is the only thing that fully accounts for the faith and proclamation of the primitive Church. The apostles were men transformed by their experience of the risen Christ. No other explanation suffices for the extraordinary events that followed Easter Sunday and Pentecost.

Now, as then, the only effective proof of the resurrection is a living faith. The resurrection remains an event which transforms and is transforming. A community which proclaims only a biological resuscitation of a corpse which lived some 2000 years ago is, at best, an historical anachronism or a curiosity piece.

The risen Lord can only be experienced today, as he was in Palestine, in the breaking of the bread—as men break bread with one another and give hope to those without hope, joy to those without peace, justice to those without rights. The Church, as the *risen* Body of Christ, must be precisely this kind of community—a community in which men can experience the risen Christ.

This is what the resurrection of Jesus is all about. It means that God the Father has crowned with glory the life and ministry of Jesus of Nazareth. The resurrection reveals that he is more than a good and decent man, more even than the greatest of men. The risen Christ is the *unique* and *ultimate* exemplar for all human life and history. His Gospel and the Kingdom of God which he came to proclaim and inaugurate have become the lynch-pin of human history. Everything is subordinate to the task of realizing and extending this Kingdom, and nothing makes sense apart from it.

The risen Christ is no longer an entombed Christ. Because he is risen, his activities know no limits. The Church, which is his risen Body, must follow her Lord out of the tomb and into the city where the unfinished business of the Kingdom awaits her.

DISCUSSION QUESTIONS

What place has the resurrection of Jesus had in your own Christian attitudes? If Jesus had not risen from the dead, would it really make any difference? Does it disturb you, as it apparently disturbs many other Catholics, to read the words, ". . . and it is the Father who raised Jesus from the dead. . ."?

Many Catholics reject attempts, such as appear in this chapter, to rethink the doctrine of the resurrection. Why do you think there is such resistance? Do you see any connection between their views on Church reform and their views

on contemporary social and political issues? If
so, how do you expain this?

By reason of the resurrection, God the Father
made Jesus the Lord of history, and the central
affirmation of faith in the primitive Church was
"Jesus is Lord." What idea do you have in mind
when you use the word "Lord" or "Our Lord"?
Do you think that many Catholics, even now, do
not fully acknowledge the humanity of Jesus? If
so, what implications does this have?

Dietrich Bonhoeffer thought that Jesus Christ
could be presented to a religionless world as "the
man for others." Do you agree? Does this phrase
tend to de-emphasize his uniqueness? When all
is said and done, what *is* so special about the
carpenter's son, Jesus of Nazareth?

> *Blessed be the God and Father of our Lord
> Jesus Christ, who has blessed us in Christ with
> every spiritual blessing in the heavenly places,
> even as he chose us in him before the founda-
> tion of the world, that we should be holy and
> blameless before him. He destined us in love
> to be his sons through Jesus Christ, accord-
> ing to the purpose of his will, to the praise of
> his glorious grace which he freely bestowed
> on us in the Beloved. In him we have re-
> demption through his blood, the forgiveness*

of our trespasses, according to the riches of his grace which he lavished upon us. For he has made known to us in all wisdom and insight the mystery of his will, according to his purpose which he set forth in Christ as a plan for the fulness of time, to unite and all things in him, things in heaven and things on earth.

Eph. 1:3-10

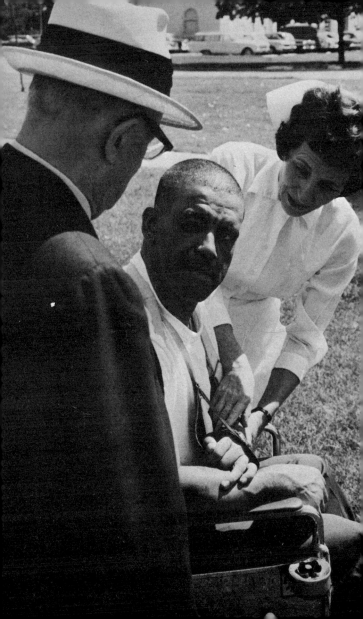

Chapter Five

THE ASCENSION—NOT A FLIGHT
BUT A CHALLENGE

"I will not leave you desolate; I will come to you. Yet a little while, and the world will see me no more, but you will see me; because I live, you will live also. In that day you will know that I am in my Father, and you in me, and I in you. He who has my commandments and keeps them, he it is who loves me; and he who loves me will be loved by my Father, and I will love him and manifest myself to him.
John 14:18-21

Those who have had the opportunity to tour the Holy Land will recall the moment when, atop the Mount of Olives, the guide dutifully called attention to the footprints of the ascended Christ. Imbedded in rock, they mark for all time the spot from which Jesus left the earth to return to his Father in heaven. There are any number of similar items in the Holy Land excursion to tax the "faith" of any man, but this one is so absurd that good-humored laughter is the only sensible reaction. Am I suggesting here that we Christians are not required to believe that Jesus was taken *up* into heaven after forty days of random post-resurrection activity? If so, what is it that we celebrate each year on the feast of the Ascension? A myth? A fairy tale? Religious nonsense?

The Ascension is in the same category as the resurrection of Jesus. It was a real, but not an historical event, i.e., not an event in space and time. If a photographer were present at that moment, there would have been no one there to photograph. First of all, how could the Ascension of Jesus be a spatial reality? If the real, physical body of the crucified Lord were literally taken

up into heaven, does that mean that now, after
some 2000 years, his body is somewhere beyond
our solar system, in another galaxy? "Of course
not!" the good Christian indignantly retorts. And
yet the same person would probably resent the
proposal that the Ascension was not a literal event
at all. Well, then, did Jesus literally go *up* before
his disciples' eyes, but when he finally got out of
sight, the event was no longer physical and God
called the whole thing off? Can we really have it
both ways?

Secondly, was the Ascension an event in time?
More precisely: was it something that happened
forty days after Easter? The problem of "dating"
the Ascension is a problem of biblical analysis.
We cannot go into that question here, except
to indicate that contemporary biblical studies in-
clude the Ascension of Jesus as part of his resurrection. They are two aspects of one and the
same reality. The forty-days-after-Easter idea is
a construction of St. Luke, but the reasons are
beyond the range of this booklet.*

If the Ascension is not, after all, an event that
can be circumscribed by space and time, what
possible meaning can it have? As we saw already,
the fundamental confession of Christian faith
affirms that "Jesus is Lord," and it is the resur-

*Readers may consult J. L. McKenzie's *Dictionary of the Bible*,
(Bruce, Milwaukee, Wisc.) or J. M. Robinson's article in *The
Interpreter's Dictionary of the Bible*, (Abingdon, Nashville,
Tenn.) Vol. I.

rection-ascension event which establishes his lordship (Phil. 2:5-11). To bring out more of the inexhaustible meaning of this event, we may say that by his resurrection, Jesus becomes the principle of new life; by the Ascension, he becomes sovereign over all creation. The ascended Christ is the Lord of history. This means that nothing in human life or history has any meaning apart from the risen and exalted Lord. This Jesus of Nazareth who was crucified on Calvary is the unique and ultimate exemplar for all human existence. There is no other.

To affirm this is to affirm the lordship of Jesus. This is what it means to be a Christian. The Ascension signifies that Jesus is now radically in control of all the principalities and powers of the universe: the forces of greed, arrogance, prejudice, bigotry, violence, dishonesty, maliciousness, apathy, superstition, cynicism, hatred. The Ascension announces the subjugation of all these powers to Jesus, the Lord. His power, the power of love, can ultimately conquer all.

The Ascension likewise is a summons to the Church to bring all things under the sovereign will of God. The Christian community is called forward to take hold of the reins alongside, and in collaboration with, its risen Lord. As a story about a going-up into the sky, the Ascension is a sedative for a community which longs for the sleep of complacency, indifference, apathy, and non-involvement, and which looks upon its heavenly reward essentially in terms of "eternal rest." But as the realization of the lordship of Jesus, the Ascension is a challenge to emerge from slumber into a creative and militant implementation of the Gospel.

This last sentence can itself have a soporific (because abstract) quality to it. What does it mean concretely, for us here and now?

It means that Christ did not leave the earth once and for all at his Ascension, to be present with us now only in Holy Communion and in the tabernacle. The Second Vatican Council reminded us that, even at Mass, Christ is present not only in the eucharistic species of bread and wine, but also in the priest, the word contained in the Scripture readings, and particularly in the community which has gathered together for worship (c.f. Mt. 18:20). Indeed, it is for the sake of his presence in the community—the entire human community—that we have his presence in the Church, the Eucharist, and the Word.

The message and meaning of the Ascension is, then, that Christ is now present in all of mankind—under the sacrament of the neighbor. This presence is dramatized most effectively in the Lord's own parable of the sheep and the goats: "Lord, when did we see thee hungry and feed

thee, or thirsty and give thee drink? And when did we see thee a stranger and welcome thee, or naked and clothe thee? And when did we see thee sick or in prison and visit thee?" And the King will answer them, "Truly, I say to you, as you did it to one of the least of these my brethren, you did it to me." (And those on his left hand will ask,) "When did we see thee hungry or thirsty or a stranger or naked or sick or in prison, and did not minister to thee?" And he will answer them: "Truly, I say to you, as you did it not to one of the least of these, you did it not to me" (Mt. 25:37-46).

The Christian is the one who must publicly announce, disclose, and release the presence of Christ in the world. The Church of every age must place itself under the judgment of the Gospel and, more specifically, under the judgment of the parable of the sheep and the goats. The Father will put his challenge to the whole Christian community: Did my Church hasten the coming of the Kingdom? Did it erect signs of hope and promise in the midst of frustration, disillusionment, and despair? Did it offer itself as a rallying-point, "a drum-major for justice" in a world of fear and prejudice, of callous indifference and disruptive hate?

Recent national opinion surveys and a Presidential commission report have given us some idea of the work that remains to be done, in our country alone, if the challenge of the Ascension is to be met. A Harris poll indicates that only a threadbare margin of white Americans approve of urban redevelopment in our slums (45-43 percent), but an overwhelming number (63-23 percent) oppose higher taxes to pay for this.

The number of white Americans who feel alienated from our society has risen from 24 to 30 percent since 1966, while the percentage of black alienation has risen from 34 to 54 percent over the same period.

The number of white Americans who feel that other people do not really understand what it is to live as they must live is now at 25 percent. A full 66 percent of black Americans feel this way.

There are 55 percent of white Americans and 32 percent of black Americans who admit to possessing guns in their homes, and roughly half of them said they would use these weapons in a riot, if pressed.

The Report of the National Advisory Commission on Civil Disorders (the Kerner Report) insists that the basic cause of trouble in our cities is white racism—prejudice and discriminatory practices on the part of the white community against the black community. Meanwhile, a Gallup poll reveals that 57 percent of the Catholics interviewed and 52 percent of the Protestants think that "the churches (should) keep out of political and social matters."

Skilled politicians, who are not usually accused of naive romanticism, have learned to take these polls seriously. National political parties decide upon their Presidential nominees with a firm eye toward Gallup and Harris. There is no reason for the Church to adopt a more skeptical attitude than the practical politician.

What these recent polls suggest is that a great many Church members do not know what the Gospel is all about.

DISCUSSION QUESTIONS

Have you ever really tried to think through the mystery of the Ascension? How did you picture it to yourself? Does it still make sense to you?

What significance has this doctrine of the Ascension had for you until now? What do you think it means for most Catholics?

Does the Gallup poll accurately reflect the opinions of Catholics of your own acquaintance? Do you think that most Catholics know that the Church was always involved in the social apostolate (e.g., through the papal encyclicals of Leo XIII and Pius XI)? Why, then, do so many of them reject the renewed emphasis on social and political involvement?

> *So then the Lord Jesus, after he had spoken to them, was taken up into heaven, and sat down at the right hand of God. And they went forth and preached everywhere, while the Lord worked with them and confirmed the message by the signs that attended it. Amen.*

Mark 16:19-20

Chapter Six

"SERVANTS OF THE BRETHREN"

*"I hate, I despise your feasts, and I take
no delight in your solemn assemblies.*

*Even though you offer me your burnt offer-
ings and cereal offerings, I will not accept
them, and the peace offerings of your fatted
beasts I will not look upon.*

*Take away from me the noise of your songs;
to the melody of your harps I will not listen.*

*But let justice roll down like waters, and
righteousness like an everflowing stream.*

Amos 5:21-24

Former U.S. Senator Paul Douglas, of Illinois, recently remarked: "Perhaps the chief effect of the organized church was to inoculate the great mass of Western mankind with such a mild dose of Christianity as to make them immune to the real thing."

Is it possible that the Church, which exists for the sake of the Kingdom of God, has unintentionally achieved the opposite result? Is it possible that the Church's preaching of the Gospel has simply provided Western man a pious, religiously flavored vocabulary with which to clothe a basic apathy, indifference, or hard-heartedness?

Is it possible that the Church has unintentionally made itself into a comfortable refuge, a warm and reassuringly appointed shelter within which men can attain a certain feeling of well-being and righteousness? Has it, in reality, served to insulate and isolate its members from their human responsibilities by reminding them that this is but "a vale of tears" which is not ultimately worth our blood and sweat?

Is it possible that the Church could have struggled to form a genuinely Christian community and yet produced too often a bigoted, ethnically-conscious ghetto which hoards guns, enters into real estate covenants on racist terms, and threatens economic reprisals upon those who presume to confront them with the Gospel?

I have been suggesting throughout this booklet that it is not really possible to speak about the Church in isolation from the rest of theology. When we say something about the Church, we are also saying something, at least indirectly, about God, Christ, the redemption, grace, original sin, and other elements of the Christian faith. And if our ideas about some of these doctrines are distorted, our understanding of the nature and mission of the Church will be affected proportionately. This, of course, has happened. So, too, our understanding of the ordained priesthood within the Church will reflect our prior attitudes toward these related areas of Christian doctrine, and particularly our ideas about Christ and the Church itself. If the Church is understood as the "means of salvation" dispensing the "grace" needed to get to heaven, then the ministry of the ordained priest is reduced to sacramental administration: he is a kind of service-station attendant, to assist people to "get tanked up on grace" (an analogy that used to be in actual use in sermons). The significance of the ministry of the Church is therefore enhanced rather than diminished by attempting to view it in its largest theological context; for the ordained priesthood makes no sense apart from the priesthood of Christ, the priesthood of the Church, and the priesthood of the bishop.

Jesus was High Priest because he was, first of all, the Suffering Servant of God. He gave himself unto death for the sake of the Kingdom, in order that men might be brought together as one family under God. This is what the at-one-ment is all about. The sacrifice that he offered as High Priest was the sacrifice of himself (Heb. 7:27). He came "not to be served, but to serve and to give his life as a ransom for many" (Mk. 10:45).

The Church, as the Body of Christ, shares in this same priestly office. And we are speaking here of the whole Church, not simply of the ordained minority. (See the *Dogmatic Constitution on the Church,* art. 10.) The Church's priesthood is not exclusively liturgical or sacramental, because Christ's priesthood encompassed more than worship. He was a priest not only on the altar of the cross but throughout his whole life—when he gave sight to the blind, hearing to the deaf, life to the dead, and hope to the poor. The Church is a priestly community because it is, in the first instance, the Body of the Suffering Servant of God. Like Jesus, the Church must exercise its priesthood through a ministry of announcing, realizing, and embodying the Kingdom of God. It must be able to present itself to the world as a credible sign and instrument of the coming Kingdom of God.

It is important that we see the mission of the Church in terms of the mission of the Lord himself. Article 5 of the Second Vatican Council's *Dogmatic Constitution on the Church* makes this connection, but it was done almost as an afterthought and did not substantially influence the basic theological orientation of the whole document.

The Church must publicly proclaim that the preaching and ministry, the death and resurrection, of Jesus of Nazareth contain the key to human existence and human history. Our relationship with God is a filial one. We are neither slaves nor pawns. He loves us like a Father and wishes us to love him and one another as his faithful children. Man is no longer subservient to religious prescriptions and tribal customs. None of these can bring us to our salvation, particularly when they obstruct rather than foster the development of genuinely human values. The Church must announce, as Jesus announced before it, that God is present to human life, that he is with us as the force who can bind men together, who can reconcile what is opposed, and heal what is wounded. The Church is there to remind mankind that God is not to be grasped by some metaphysical leap but by reaching out to him in other people.

If the Church should exist as the principal lobbyist for genuinely human values and the prophetic judge of all that strikes against the human spirit, then the Church must demonstrate its commitment in action as well as in word. The Church which preaches the arrival of the Kingdom must be known as the world's "drum-major for justice," as a doer of the word. The ministry that we called in the past "the social apostolate" is essential to the life and mission of the Church. Service is not an "extra" or a preliminary to the "real" work of the Church. Giving food to the hungry and medicine to the sick, for example, should not be debased by the term "pre-evangelization." This is as much a part of the Church's mission as preaching, catechetical instruction, or sacramental celebration. The worshipping and preaching community must be a Servant Church.

If the Church preaches the Gospel of Christ without compromise and if it struggles here and now to realize this Gospel in the fabric of our contemporary political and social order, then this Church will become "the sign lifted up among the nations" (Vatican I). People will be able to look to this community and see that at least it practices what it preaches. As such, it can become a symbol of community in a world that so often rejects its responsibilities to create and deepen the bonds of friendship and fellowship among men.

When the Church turns in upon itself and seeks only to maintain its structures, it has forfeited its charter of existence. The Church makes no sense apart from the Kingdom of God. It has no reason for existence apart from its mission to announce, establish, and embody this Kingdom.

Even though its mission is outer-directed, the Church has certain needs of its own, as a community. Someone must preside over its assemblies when it gathers for the Eucharist. Someone must preach the Word of God, so that the community never loses sight of its ultimate responsibilities for the Kingdom. Someone must guide, direct, and inspire the various groupings within the Church, so that they may more effectively implement the Gospel wherever they live and work. Someone must presume to set an example for the community, lest they be tempted to retreat from the standard of Christ or be satisfied with half-hearted accommodations or hypocritical compromises.

This is the task of the ordained priesthood, and antecedently of the bishops. The Second Vatican Council calls them "servants of the brethren." Their power and authority is given to them for the sake of the Church, that they might form a genuine Christian community—a community which will, indeed, be a credible sign and an effective instrument of the Kingdom.

What ultimately marks off the bishop and the priest from the non-ordained Christian is the fact that they are professionally and sacramentally committed to the service of the Church as such: to preach the Gospel, to preside at the Eucharist, to celebrate the sacraments, to minister to the sick, to bury the dead, to instruct those who seek affiliation with the community, to educate the young and the mature in the knowledge of the Gospel, to lead and direct apostolate groups.

In a word, priesthood in the Church assists the community to become more fully what it has radically become at Baptism: the very Body of the Suffering Servant of God and our High Priest.

Those who argue in our time for a de-emphasis on the ministerial priesthood, who rejoice in the decline of vocations or in the growing number of resignations, have, in their moment of anti-clerical passion, ignored the quality and kind of leadership which only the ordained Christian is in a position to give. "And how are they to believe in him of whom they have never heard? And how are they to hear without a preacher? And how can men preach unless they are sent?" (Rom. 10:14-15).

The ordained priest is, by definition, a pro-

fessional religious leader; and by sacramental
commission, the colleague of the bishop in the
service of a particular Christian community. This
is what is distinctive about the priest: not that he
preaches the Gospel (which is his primary task),
not that he celebrates Mass, not that he visits the
sick, not that he teaches Christian doctrine—
although all of these tasks are eminently appro-
priate to the ordained ministry. The priest shares
in the bishop's threefold missionary responsibility
(just as the bishop shares in the Church's, and the
Church in Christ's): to announce the coming of
the Kingdom; to see to it that the Church struggles to initiate and to extend this Kingdom here
and now; and, finally, to form the Christian
people into a genuine community, one that can
offer itself as a credible sign of the Kingdom
and a source of authentic hope for the future of
mankind and of this world.

Spiritual power is conferred upon the priest
not for his own sake: neither for his own sanctity, nor for his own salvation. The priest is not a
kind of "super-Christian" with a flying headstart
in the race of heavenly bliss. All his power is
given to him, as the Second Vatican Council insists in several of its documents, for the sake of
the people and for the upbuilding of the Church.
And the Church exists always for the sake of
God's Kingdom.

If the priest were to become the servant of the socio-economic and political prejudices of his people rather than of the Kingdom of God, he would effectively negate his prophetic role. Sacraments may be administered in abundance; countless marriages may be "fixed up" or canonically validated; hundreds of funerals and wakes, wedding receptions and anniversary parties may have been dutifully attended. But the realization and extension of God's Kingdom would remain a dead letter. And so, too, these priestly works—good and commendable in themselves—would be a waste of time, and worse. Perhaps one important reason why so many priests are leaving the ministry is that they realize that they *have* been wasting their time.

The priest is neither village wise-man nor witch-doctor. His role makes sense only in terms of the Church which he presumes to serve, and in terms of the reign of God, which constitutes the center and goal of everything that is.

In the past, many Catholics have idealized the ordained priest to the extent that he became a kind of "super-Christian." This reflected too often a magical view of redemption and a pre-Christian view of God, sin, and grace. But Jesus came to celebrate and thereby to redeem what is authentically human. The "Going My Way" type of priest betrays a "Going My Way" type of Church.

It has no connection with the assurance of the Lord that he alone is "the Way, the Truth, and the Life."

DISCUSSION QUESTIONS

Answer the questions posed at the beginning of this chapter.

How is the role of the ordained priest changing today? Are you happy with the change? Why? What further changes will be required if the Church is to fulfill its mission in the world?

Do you think that the bishops fully appreciated the pastoral and theological changes that they were endorsing at the Second Vatican Council? Which conclusions of Vatican II do you think they have most seriously ignored? Which items do you think they have most faithfully implemented?

Do you think the Church is still necessary?

> *And James and John, the sons of Zebedee, came forward to him, and said to him, "Teacher, we want you to do for us whatever we ask of you." And he said to them, "What do you want me to do for you?" And they said to him, "Grant us to sit, one at your right hand and one at your left, in your glory. But Jesus said to them, "You do not*

know what you are asking. Are you able to drink the cup that I drink, or to be baptized with the baptism with which I am baptized?" And they said to him, "We are able." And Jesus said to them, "The cup that I drink you will drink; and with the baptism with which I am baptized, you will be baptized; but to sit at my right hand or at my left is not mine to grant, but it is for those for whom is has been prepared." And when the ten heard it, they began to be indignant at James and John. And Jesus called them to him and said to them, "You know that those who are supposed to rule over the Gentiles lord it over them, and their great men exercise authority over them. But it shall not be so among you; but whoever would be great among you must be your servant, and whoever would be first among you must be slave of all. For the Son of man also came not to be served but to serve, and to give his life as a ransom for many."

Mark 10:35-45

Chapter Seven

"CALLED TO BE HOLY"

Above all hold unfailing your love for one another, since love covers a multitude of sins. Practice hospitality ungrudgingly to one another. As each has received a gift, employ it for one another as good stewards of God's varied grace: whoever speaks, as one who utters oracles of God; whoever renders service, as one who renders it by the strength which God supplies; in order that in everything God may be glorified through Jesus Christ. To him belong glory and dominion for ever and ever. Amen.

1 Peter 4:8-11

Holiness is the most basic requirement of the Christian life. Apart from genuine sanctity, no project, program or policy of the Church can achieve final success.

One should normally expect a religious principle of this sort to elicit immediate endorsement, without further comment or debate. How does one, be he reformer or opponent of changes in the Church, comfortably resist the call to Christian holiness as a matter of primary and central importance?

But this is precisely the problem. We have not had nearly enough comment or debate about Christian spirituality in terms of the best and most advanced theological understanding. And even where there has been fruitful and lively discussion, its effects have yet to be felt far beyond the academic or specifically religious circles where it originated.

In the past we may have too often confused "holiness" with various forms of narrowmindedness, puritanical or Jansenistic behavior, scrupulosity, introversion, or any number of psychological aberrations. We may have canonized mental illness and scorned the healthy and the mature under the guise of condemning selfishness, pride, arrogance or irreverence.

And in our own time, we may be yielding, almost by default, the language and vocabulary of "holiness" to the ecclesiastical resistance movement—to those who effectively delay or obstruct change by challenging the integrity and motivation of those who propose it and by paternalistically prescribing prayer and penance as an antidote to theological and pastoral frustration.

In Sacred Scripture, and particularly in the Old Testament, holiness is portrayed as an essential quality of God. His holiness is that which makes God what he is. And, as St. John assures us, God is Love.

Throughout the history of Israel, God manifested his holiness by his righteousness, his disdain for and judgment upon sin, his merciful deliverance of his people from danger and misfortunes, and by his constancy and fidelity to the covenant which he had established with them.

And man is holy insofar as he shares in this essential reality of God, which is love. Holiness cannot be limited, therefore, to specifically religious activity. Israel did not show forth its holiness through worship alone.

Israel's holiness is always related to its task in history. Israel is a holy nation because it is a people set apart by God's choice in order to fulfill a special mission in the world.

In the New Testament the quality of holiness is applied directly to the Church (1 Peter 2:9), and in the Acts of the Apostles the Christian community is referred to as "the saints." The Church receives this holiness through faith, Baptism, union with Christ, and through the righteousness which results from such union (Rom. 6:19).

It is the Holy Spirit who allows us to address God as "Father" and one another as "brother" and "sister." "Do you not know," St. Paul asked the Corinthians, "that your body is a temple of the Holy Spirit within you, which you have from God?" (1 Cor. 6:19). There can be no barrier, therefore, between the sacred and the profane, between the spiritual and the worldly. The Spirit of Christ has made all things new, because "if the Spirit of him who raised Jesus from the dead dwells in you, then he who raised Jesus Christ from the dead will also bring to life your mortal bodies because of his Spirit who dwells in you" (Rom. 8:11). And the Spirit dwells wherever men become friends, wherever the Gospel of Jesus Christ is realized and put into practice. This occurs wherever there is "love, joy, peace, patience, kindness, goodness, faithfulness, gentle-

ness, self-control" (Gal. 5:22-23), for these are
the fruits of the Holy Spirit, the signs of his presence. This is the "good news" that we bear: that
God is present among us through his Spirit, reconciling, healing, uniting.

The primary effect of Christian holiness is the
obligation of meeting Christian moral standards.
Holiness is necessary for the Christian community
if it expects to hasten the day when God's Kingdom will be realized throughout all of creation
(2 Pt. 3:11).

Thus, the Church manifests its holiness when
it faithfully executes its mission to realize and to
extend the reign and rule of God in the world.
And the individual member of the Church manifests his holiness by an active and uncompromising participation in the mission of the entire
Christian community.

We are not speaking here, of course, about
lobbying against liberalized divorce laws or for
prayer in the public schools. These are peripheral
items compared to the great issues of peace and
justice for all. The growth of the Kingdom is not
measured by the political achievements of the
Church, on behalf of its own interests. It is a
matter instead of the growth and development of
genuinely human values, the kind of values en-
dorsed in Pope John XXIII's *Mater et Magistra*
and *Pacem in Terris,* in Pope Paul VI's *Popu-*

lorum Progressio, and in Vatican II's *Pastoral Constitution on the Church in the Modern World.*

Holiness, therefore, is not exclusively, nor even primarily, a matter of code and cult. Holiness may indeed be measured at times by the number of moments spent in prayer before the Blessed Sacrament, but it is more likely to be measured by the moments spent with a sick or troubled friend.

Holiness may be measured by the discreet and respectful silence in the face of unjust criticism or reprisals, but it is, at least, as likely to be measured by one's frank and outspoken denunciation of social injustice, wherever and by whomever it may be practiced.

Holiness is wholeness, to use the phrase of Josef Goldbrunner. The one who is most fully human is the one who most closely approximates the holiness of God. It is the free and mature man who is the holy man. He is both free and mature because he is not ruled by ambition, superstition, mythologies, prejudice, self-centeredness, or arrogance. And he is holy because he is genuinely free—liberated from these multiple forms of slavery by the One who came to set all men free.

The authentic Christian, and hence the genuinely human person, is one who is capable of loving other people, who is sensitive to their needs, who instinctively and spontaneously comes forward to bear their burdens, who is not satisfied until the demands of charity and justice have been fulfilled for every human being. But he realizes that this form of behavior is beyond his own reach, that he can live this Gospel-life only because God is present to human relationships where, underneath these relationships, he offers us his own love. We dare to love one another because he has loved us first in Christ (1 Jn. 4: 10-11). It is *in response to* his love that we seek to create community with others, and it is *in response to* his call that we Christians dare to offer our lives as a sign (however tentative) of the Kingdom (1 Pet. 4:8-11).

In a real sense, therefore, Christian *morality* is a matter of Christian *responsibility:* a life fashioned in response to the presence of God in human relationships and to his call to share the mission of the Church. Life is not some kind of sporting event arranged and managed for God's personal entertainment, where the life-and-death issues are a matter of rule-keeping and rule-breaking. Nor is it really helpful to employ the various analogies drawn from military discipline and practice. (Yet how often do Catholics appeal to military analogies when speaking in defense of authority, priestly loyalty, or, indeed, even the sacrament of Confirmation!) We need not endorse every aspect of the so-called "new morality" to suggest that its basic criticisms of the "old morality" are valid and its fundamental orientation is sound.

Morality is a matter of responding to the call of God to build his Kingdom, to establish among men a community of peace and friendship, of justice and liberty for all. The supreme value is God's Kingdom. No rule, no custom, no commandment can ever be allowed to obstruct or obscure this goal. Everything is relativized by the injunction to "seek first the Kingdom of God." To absolutize anything but the Kingdom is to absolutize something less than divine, and this is blasphemous and idolatrous. To the extent that the Church has ever placed its own needs ahead of the needs of the larger human community, she has absolutized herself and therefore made herself into an idol. To the extent that any single Christian puts the "salvation of his own immortal soul" ahead of the legitimate needs of his fellow man, he, too, has made himself into an idol. And the Lord warned us that the two great commandments are really one and the same. To ignore the claims of our neighbor is to put strange gods before us.

DISCUSSION QUESTIONS

What do you mean when you refer to someone as a "very devout Catholic" or a "very holy priest"? What do you think most Catholics mean when they use these terms?

What role has ethnic tradition played in the formation of Christian consciences? Do you think that the moral attitudes of Catholics are influenced as much sometimes by their national backgrounds as by their knowledge and assimilation of the Gospel?

Does the distinction between "natural" and "supernatural" mean very much to you? Do you think this distinction has created any problems in the formation of proper Christian attitudes? Do you think that there is a tendency today to de-emphasize the "supernatural"?

What disturbs you most about the "new morality"? Why does it disturb you? What disturbs you most about the "old morality"? Why does it disturb you?

How does Christian morality differ from the kind of morality that every human being is expected to follow? If there is a difference, where is it? If there is not any essential difference, then why be a Christian?

> *Say to those who are of a fearful heart, "Be strong, fear not! Behold, your God will come with vengeance, with the recompense of God. He will come and save you."*

*Then the eyes of the blind shall be opened,
and the ears of the deaf unstopped;*

*then shall the lame man leap like a hart,
and the tongue of the dumb sing for joy.*

For waters shall break forth in the wilderness, and streams in the desert;

*the burning sand shall become a pool, and
the thirsty ground springs of water; the haunt
of jackals shall become a swamp, the grass
shall become reeds and rushes.*

*And a highway shall be there, and it shall
be called the Holy Way; the unclean shall not
pass over it, and fools shall not err therein.*

*No lion shall be there, nor shall any ravenous beast come up on it; they shall not be
found there, but the redeemed shall walk
there.*

*And the ransomed of the Lord shall return, and come to Zion with singing; everlasting joy shall be upon their heads; they
shall obtain joy and gladness, and sorrow and
sighing shall flee away.*

Isaiah 35:4-10

Chapter Eight

"COME, LORD JESUS!"

And Jesus said to them, "The sons of this age marry and are given in marriage; but those who are accounted worthy to attain to that age and to the resurrection from the dead neither marry nor are given in marriage, for they cannot die any more, because they are equal to angels and are sons of God, being sons of the resurrection. But that the dead are raised, even Moses showed, in the passage about the bush, where he calls the Lord the God of Abraham and the God of Isaac and the God of Jacob. Now he is not God of the dead, but of the living; for all live to him."

Luke 20:34-38

The Christian community lives in expectation of the coming of its Lord. The note of vigilance and preparedness is sounded again and again throughout the pages of the New Testament. But what does this doctrine of the Second Coming really mean? Is it concerned only with some day in the far distant future when Christ will come again to wind things up, "when the heavens and the earth shall be moved and the world shall come to an end by fire"? Were this the case, the doctrine of the Second Coming would be nearly meaningless and irrelevant. Who really expects the end of the world to occur in his own lifetime? The nuclear armaments race notwithstanding, we can easily give lip-service to this doctrine and then neatly file it away in our religious treasure box.

But the Second Coming of Christ actually refers more to the present and the immediate future than to the distant beyond of history. Christ comes into our lives even now, in those multiple crises when all of us are confronted with the challenge to accept or to reject the Gospel.

Christ came unexpectedly into the life of the Good Samaritan, and he ministered to him along

that road to Jericho. He came into the life of the
Levite in the same way that same day, but the
young priest did not recognize him. Christ chooses
to encounter us both in the neighbor who is in
need and in the neighbor who reaches out to
minister to our own needs. He is in the healer
and the healed, in the peace-maker and the mili-
tarist, in the champion of human rights and in
the perpetrator of injustice. What is always distinctive about his coming is its surprising and un-
expected character: "You know not the day nor
the hour."

A re-reading of the parable of the sheep and
the goats in the twenty-fifth chapter of St. Mat-
thew's Gospel will disclose this theology in its
classic form. It is not a comfortable passage for
many of us.

"When did we see you hungry or thirsty or a
stranger or naked or sick or in prison, and did
not minister to you?" Except for the medium of
television (although its impact cannot lightly be
dismissed), most middle-class Christians are se-
curely insulated from the intrusion of those in
need, of those who have a claim upon us by reason of our common humanity and our public
acceptance of the Gospel of Jesus Christ. Few of
us ride through the poverty pockets of our cities
in order to jeer at those who are veritable pris-
oners of these ghettoes. We simply ignore them.

But our encounter with the poor, the hungry, the thirsty, and the naked Christ still occurs, although at a more sophisticated—and more obscure—level: in the voting booth. It is here that the Christian too often supports office-holders or new candidates who promise lower taxes at the expense of the poor, stiffer law enforcement procedures sometimes at the expense of the people they are designed to protect, cutbacks in federal spending (seldom in the area of peanut and cotton subsidies, inevitably in the areas of urban redevelopment, education, housing). Little escapes the long arm of rationalization. Some even attempted to justify opposition to the rat control bill that was first defeated, then passed, last year in response to the display of public outrage. In many instances, however, we "know not what we do" because we have not taken the trouble to inform ourselves on candidates and issues.

As the Gallup poll revealed some months ago, most Christians (57% of the Catholics, and 52% of the Protestants) oppose the involvement of the Church in matters of social and political consequence. They have not yet confronted the doctrine of the Second Coming of the Lord.

Throughout this booklet the stress has been placed on the social dimension of Christian life and belief. This does not mean that we should be unconcerned with the personal destiny of each individual human being. The point has been that no single person can hope to achieve salvation independently of the larger human community. The parable of the sheep and the goats reminds us that the final judgment will be made on the basis of the quality of our response to one another's needs. It is precisely in loving other people and in caring for their needs that we attain ultimate human fulfillment. And holiness, as we mentioned in the last chapter, is wholeness.

No Catholic should become so alarmed by the current ferment in theology that he begins to wonder if he has reason any longer to hope for his own salvation. Shall we all be taken up into some kind of cosmic mass? Shall we become nothing more than an impersonal dot on a huge Omega Point?

". . . No eye has seen, nor ear heard, nor the heart of man conceived, what God has prepared for those who love him" (1 Cor. 2:9). But we demonstrate our love for God in our love for one another. The epistles of St. John are themselves a brilliant commentary on the parable of the sheep and the goats. The point is clear enough: for those who strive sincerely, earnestly and with perseverance to live the Gospel of Jesus Christ, "in season and out of season, when convenient and inconvenient," God has prepared something that exceeds our highest thoughts and desires (see the Oration for the Mass of the Fifth Sunday after Pentecost). He will give us the complete fulfillment of human life in a community of mutual love and friendship. Our faith and our hope is that the Kingdom for which we are struggling here and now will be perfected for us on the last day when the Lord will come again to make all things new.

As Catholics who are troubled—or, worse still, angered and embittered—by fluctuations in the explanation and expression of Christian doctrine are usually quick to remind us, theologians are neither the source nor the norm of faith. For some of these Catholics, it may come as a surprise that theologians themselves would not only accept this point of view but would actually insist upon it.

Theology is not faith, but the reflection upon faith; and the theologian is its servant. His task is a human, fallible attempt to make sense of what we already believe about God, Christ, the Gospel, and the Church and to determine some of the implications of our belief for our life and work in this world.

It is possible, in other words, for a Christian to possess authentic faith without being particularly adept at theological reasoning. A specific Christian may know next to nothing about the Council of Chalcedon or the controversy regarding person

and nature in Jesus Christ, but he may demonstrate a genuine "knowledge" of the Lord through
his compassion and generosity in the service of
his neighbor, and through his determination to
subject all things to the reign and rule of God.

The Christian may not be able to define, much
less to defend in debate, the scholastic concept of
transubstantiation. He may never have heard of
Edward Schillebeeckx, or Piet Schoonenberg, or
any of the other contemporary theologians who
have written on the problem of the Real Presence
in the Eucharist. But he may understand, none-
theless, that in the breaking of the bread and in
the eating and drinking of the body and blood of
the Lord, he really meets the Lord of history, he
really is engrafted more deeply into the Body of
Christ, and he really does testify to the death and
resurrection of the Lord "until he comes."

Undoubtedly, this will appear to some as a
painful belaboring of the obvious. Of course,
theology and faith are not the same thing. But it
seems to be the obvious things that generate the
greatest difficulties in the contemporary Church.
It is almost as if some people feel that they must
hold their faith in abeyance each time a new
theological question is raised.

On the contrary, if the Christian has long
since closed his heart to the poor and the needy,
to the sick and the homeless, to the hostile and

the belligerent, no amount of theological discussion will clarify his faith in Jesus Christ, his understanding of sin and grace, his perception of the Lord in the Eucharist, or his concept of natural law and the law of God.

On the other hand, if the Christian has opened his heart to the Lord of the Gospel, no amount of theological debate can unsettle or disrupt his faith.

Is it merely coincidental that opposition to theological developments often emanates from those whose political judgments and attitudes reflect a posture somewhat at odds with the tradition of the Church's social teachings?

Is not the impassioned concern to preserve and defend the divinity of Christ, to use one example, simply the reverse side of a fear of attributing too much importance to the humanity of Jesus? For it is in his humanity, rather than in his divinity, that Jesus Christ comes so uncomfortably close to life. As God, he is "up there," someone to be believed in and adored—when the day and the hour are convenient. But as man, as one with us and as one of us, he can and must be met at all points. Christ comes into everything. He becomes as much a political reality as a liturgical or sacramental reality.

To be a Christian means to expect Christ to come into everything. To be a Christian means to

discern his presence here, there, and in every human crisis. To believe this demands an act of faith. Not to believe it makes life a good deal more simple and a good deal more comfortable.

The Christian who wants to go to the mat over the definitions of papal infallibility, the divinity of Christ, the Real Presence, the existence of hell, the importance of the Blessed Virgin, or any number of similar issues, should first check his own emotional and intellectual barometer in the area of Gospel ethics. He may find that the involvement of Christians in the various movements for peace, racial justice, the alleviation of poverty, and other related areas of conflict is personally far more disturbing than the suggestion of some theologian that perhaps transubstantiation is neither the best way nor the only way of understanding the presence of the Lord in the Eucharist.

Is it not possible that the real problem is there —in the area of Christian mission rather than in the area of Christian ideology? What is breaking up in the Catholic Church is not authentic Christian faith or doctrinal orthodoxy, but the culturally-conditioned idea that Christianity is essentially a white, middle-class, socially respectable religion. No idea conflicts more openly with the Gospel than this one.

When all is said and done, our faith remains

in the Lordship of Jesus Christ. Whatever our
theologies, the Christian community will continue to affirm that he is the unique and ultimate
pattern for all human life and history, that nothing shall escape his sovereignty, that nothing can
separate us from his love and from the power of
his Gospel. Jesus is the Lord, and there is no
other. But only those who can find him in other
men and women—in the poor, the sick, the
needy, the oppressed, those with whom we live
and work—know the real meaning of that confession of faith.

No theologian can really improve upon the
parable of the Good Samaritan or the parable of
the sheep and the goats (Mt. 25). The scandal
of the Gospel resides there. Theology merely tries
to make some sense of this strange message—by
constantly disengaging it from the "beliefs" that
mortal men so often substitute for it.

DISCUSSION QUESTIONS

How have you pictured the Second Coming of
Christ? Have you really thought about it at all
before now? How can our ideas about the Second Coming be influenced by our ideas about
God, Christ, and the Church?

What do you find objectionable about the
idea that Heaven is a reward for "being good"

and Hell a punishment for "being bad"? Trace these ideas back to more basic ideas about God, Christ, the redemption, the Church, and the sacraments.

Can you begin to outline a theology of Purgatory and Hell in the light of the theology proposed throughout this booklet? What about Limbo?

Do you agree that the real stumbling-block for most Catholics is the social implication of the Gospel? Why do you think this is so? How can any Christian really do anything about it?

Do you think younger people will be prepared to take the Church more seriously if this connection between the Gospel and life is more consistently and emphatically drawn?

> *"I Jesus have sent my angel to you with this testimony for the churches. I am the root and the offspring of David, the bright morning star." The Spirit and the Bride say, "Come." And let him who is thirsty come, let him who desires take the water of life without price. I warn every one who hears the words of the prophecy of this book: if any one adds to them, God will add to him the plagues described in this book, and if any one takes away from the words of the book of this prophecy, God will take away his share in the tree of life and in the holy city, which are*

described in this book. He who testifies to these things says, "Surely I am coming soon." Amen. Come, Lord Jesus! The grace of the Lord Jesus be with all the saints. Amen.

Apoc. 22:16-21

BIBLIOGRAPHY

1. A NEW CATECHISM: CATHOLIC FAITH FOR ADULTS, K. Smyth, trans. (New York: Herder & Herder, 1967). The best one-volume synthesis of contemporary Catholic theology.

2. Robinson, John A. T., BUT THAT I CAN'T BELIEVE! (New York: New American Library, 1967). A book of popular and illuminating essays on various traditional doctrines.

3. McBrien, Richard P., DO WE NEED THE CHURCH? (New York: Harper & Row, 1969). Develops at much greater length and depth some of the themes considered in this booklet, particularly the material in chapter VI.

4. Macquarrie, John, PRINCIPLES OF CHRISTIAN THEOLOGY (New York: Scribners, 1966). The best one-volume work in systematic theology. Not for beginners.

5. Marty, Martin, and Peerman, Dean, eds., NEW THEOLOGY, NO. 1,2,3,4, and 5 (New York: Macmillan, 1964 ff.). Contains reprints of some of the most important essays that have appeared in various religious publications during the previous year.